How Do Space Vehicles Work?

Buffy Silverman

Lerner Publications Company

Minneapolis

To Jeff, whose boyhood love of space sparked a lifelong love of science

Lerner Publications Company
A division of Lerner Publishing Group, Inc.
241 First Avenue North
Minneapolis, MN 55401 U.S.A.

Website address: www.lernerbooks.com

Library of Congress Cataloging-in-Publication Data

Silverman, Buffy.
    How do space vehicles work? / by Buffy Silverman.
        pages   cm. — (Lightning Bolt Books™ — How Flight Works)
    Includes index.
    ISBN 978-0-7613-8971-2 (lib. bdg. : alk. paper)
    1. Space vehicles — Juvenile literature. I. Title.
    TL795.515.S55 2013
    629.44'1 — dc23   2012019111

Manufactured in the United States of America
1 — BP — 12/31/12

Table of Contents

On the Launchpad

A railcar carries a Soyuz spacecraft. The car brings it to a launchpad. The spacecraft will take astronauts to the International Space Station. Astronauts live and work there.

Some space vehicles, like the Soyuz, carry people. Others carry machines.

A rocket and a capsule make up the spacecraft. The rocket will launch the capsule into space. The crew will ride in the capsule.

A machine lifts the spacecraft.

Many people
check the
spacecraft.
They practice
the jobs they
will do during
the launch.

Workers load the rocket with fuel. Spacecraft need energy to reach space. The energy comes from burning fuel.

Tanks in the Soyuz are filled with liquid fuel.

The rocket also carries oxygen. Fuel needs this gas to burn.

Oxygen is a gas in the air. The rocket must carry oxygen because there is no air in space.

The crew enters the capsule.
The final hours tick down on
the countdown clock.
Time for blastoff!

Rocket engines turn fuel into hot gas. Gas shoots out the back of the rocket.

The rocket also shoots out flames as the engines burn fuel.

The hot gas pushes the rocket.
The rocket soars up.

The force that pushes a rocket is called thrust.

Gravity pulls on the spacecraft.
Gravity is a force. It pulls
things to Earth.

Gravity pulls you
down when you jump.

How does a spacecraft keep from being pulled back to Earth?

It speeds away. It travels more than 4 miles (7 kilometers) per second to reach space. Gravity is much weaker there.

Four boosters make up the first stage.

The rocket has three sections. They are called stages. Each stage lifts the spacecraft for part of the launch.

Each stage burns its fuel.
Then it falls away. The rocket
has less weight to lift.

The second stage falls
away high above Earth.

Soon the capsule splits from the rocket. It has reached space.

This blue haze is the atmosphere. It is the air around Earth. Space is beyond it.

In Orbit

The capsule travels
through space.
It orbits Earth.

Orbit means "to
travel around
something."

Try to launch a ball into orbit. Throw it hard, and it travels far. But Earth's gravity pulls on it. The ball curves and falls down.

Gravity pulls on a spacecraft in orbit too. The spacecraft is falling. But it travels very fast. The curve of its fall matches the curve of Earth. So it stays in orbit.

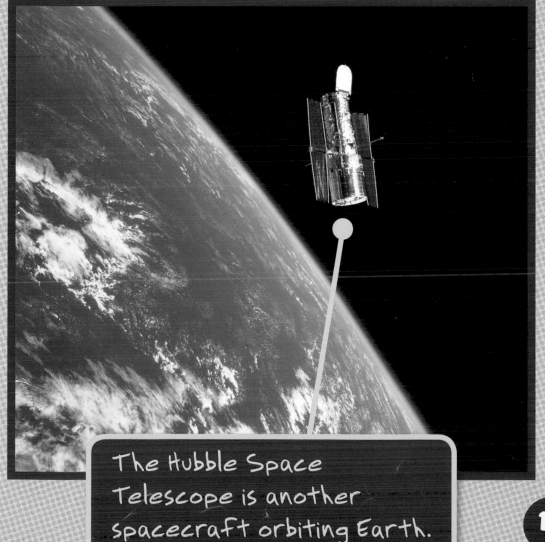

The Hubble Space Telescope is another spacecraft orbiting Earth.

There is no air in space. The temperature can be very hot or cold. A spacecraft keeps the crew warm or cool. It carries air, food, and water.

A spacecraft's solar panels make electricity from sunlight.

The space station orbits Earth every ninety minutes.

The space station also orbits Earth. The capsule reaches it after two days.

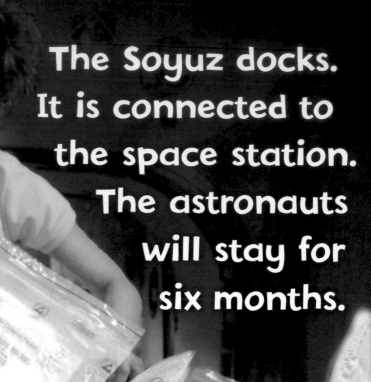

The Soyuz docks.
It is connected to
the space station.
The astronauts
will stay for
six months.

FWD

There is little gravity
inside the space station.
People can float around!

Returning to Earth

Other astronauts have worked on the space station for many months. They return to Earth in the Soyuz.

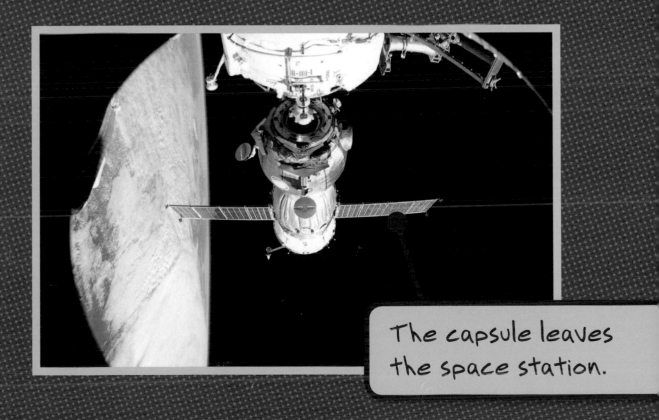

The capsule leaves the space station.

The crew fires rockets to slow the capsule in space. It falls out of orbit. Gravity pulls it to Earth.

Astronauts don't have much room inside the capsule.

The ends of the capsule drop off. Only the middle part will return to Earth.

25

The capsule rubs against air
as it enters Earth's atmosphere.
This rubbing is called friction.

Friction heats the
outside of a spacecraft.
A heat shield keeps the
spacecraft from burning.

Friction slows the speeding spacecraft. Parachutes slow it more. It floats safely to its landing spot.

Parts of a Space Vehicle

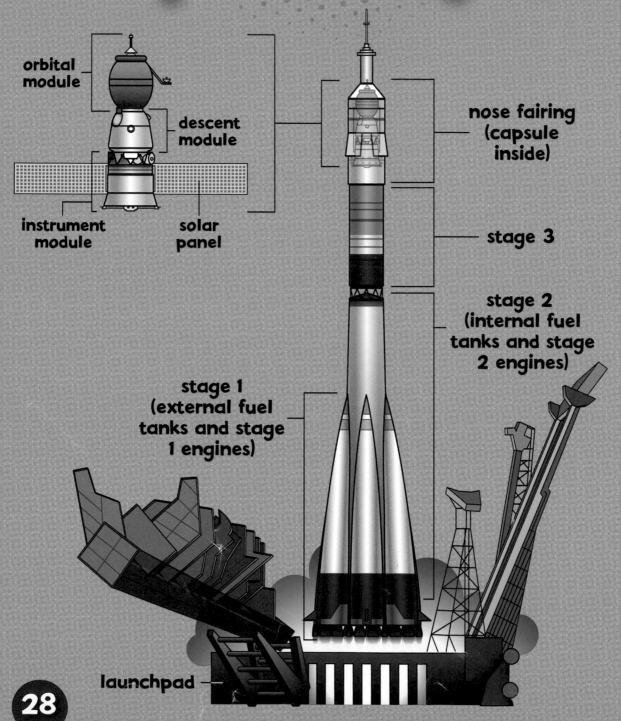

orbital module

descent module

instrument module

solar panel

nose fairing (capsule inside)

stage 3

stage 2 (internal fuel tanks and stage 2 engines)

stage 1 (external fuel tanks and stage 1 engines)

launchpad

Fun Facts

- The United States used space vehicles called space shuttles from 1981 to 2011. The shuttles carried astronauts on more than 130 missions. Since 2012, the space shuttles are at museums.

- Most spacecraft do not carry people. They are unmanned. Weather satellites are one type. They orbit Earth and take pictures. The pictures help scientists predict weather.

- A new unmanned spacecraft landed on Mars in 2012. Others have landed there before. They send pictures and information back to Earth.

- Some spacecraft are no longer in use but are still in orbit. So are bits of paint, fuel, and dust. All this is called space junk.

Glossary

astronaut: a person trained to travel in space

atmosphere: the layer of air that surrounds Earth

engine: a machine that changes fuel into motion

force: a push or pull that lifts something, starts it moving, or holds it in place

friction: the rubbing of one object against another

fuel: gasoline or another substance burned to make heat and run engines

gravity: a force that pulls objects together

rocket: a type of engine that expels hot gases out an open end at high speed

stage: a section of a rocket that carries its own fuel and engine

thrust: a force that pushes an aircraft or rocket in the air

Further Reading

Kid Zone: International Space Station
http://solc.gsfc.nasa.gov/kids3/kids3.html

Kops, Deborah. *Exploring Space Robots.* Minneapolis: Lerner Publications Company, 2012.

NASA Picture Dictionary
http://www.nasa.gov/audience /forstudents/k-4/dictionary/index.html

NASA Space Place Live
http://spaceplace.nasa.gov/http://spaceplace.nasa .gov/space-place-live/#/review/space-place-live /shows/ep008/spl.swf

Tieck, Sarah. *Astronauts.* Edina, MN: Abdo Publishing Company, 2012.

Waxman, Laura Hamilton. *Exploring the International Space Station.* Minneapolis: Lerner Publications Company, 2012.

Index

Photo Acknowledgments

The images in this book are used with the permission of: © SpaceX, pp. 1, 31; NASA/Bill Ingalls, pp. 2, 4, 5, 11, 14, 27; © Patrick Aventurier/Getty Images, p. 6; NASA/Carla Cioffi, p. 7; NASA/Victor Zelentsov, p. 8; Carla Cioffi/DPA/Picture-Alliance/Newscom, p. 9; NASA/Bill Ingalls/Carla Cioffi, p. 10; © iStockphoto.com/Kristina Serulic, p. 12; Shamil Zhumatov/Reuters/Newscom, p. 13; © Ron Miller, pp. 15, 25, 26; Nasa, pp. 16, 17, 20, 23; © Anatols/Dreamstime.com, p. 18; © Stocktrek Images/Getty Images, p. 19; NASA/JCS, pp. 21, 22; © Sergei Remezov/AFP/Getty Images, p. 24; © Laura Westlund/Independent Picture Service, p. 28; NASA/KSC, p. 30.

Front cover: NASA/JSC.

Main body text set in Johann Light 30/36.